I0482885

The Key Facts™ on

Bangladesh

Essential Information on Bangladesh

By Patrick W. Nee

The Internationalist®

www.internationalist.com

The Internationalist®

International Business, Investment, and Travel

Published by:

The Internationalist Publishing Company

96 Walter Street/ Suite 200

Boston, MA 02131, USA

Tel: 617-354-7722

www.internationalist.com

PN@internationalist.com

The Internationalist is a Registered Trademark. "Key Facts" and "The Internationalist Business Guides" are Trademarks of The Internationalist Publishing Company.

All Rights are reserved under International, Pan-American, and Pan-Asian Conventions. No part of this book may be reproduced in any form without the written permission of the publisher. All rights vigorously enforced

Table Of Contents

Chapter 1: Background

Muslim conversions and settlement in the region now referred to as Bangladesh began in the 10th century, primarily from Arab and Persian traders and preachers. Europeans began to set up trading posts in the area in the 16th century. Eventually the area known as Bengal, primarily Hindu in the western section and mostly Muslim in the eastern half, became part of British India. Partition in 1947 resulted in an eastern wing of Pakistan in the Muslim-majority area, which became East Pakistan. Calls for greater autonomy and animosity between the eastern and western wings of Pakistan led to a Bengali independence movement. That movement, led by the Awami League (AL) and supported by India, won independence for Bangladesh in 1971, although at least 300,000 civilians died in the process. The post-independence, AL government faced daunting challenges and in 1975 was overthrown by the military, triggering a series of military coups that resulted in a military-backed government and subsequent creation of the Bangladesh Nationalist Party (BNP). That government also ended in a coup in 1981, followed by military-backed rule until democratic elections in 1991. The BNP and AL have alternately held power since then, with the exception of a military-backed, emergency caretaker regime that suspended parliamentary elections planned for January 2007 in an effort to reform the political system and root out corruption. That government returned the country to fully democratic rule in December 2008 with the election of the AL and Prime Minister Sheikh HASINA. In January 2014, the AL won the national election by an overwhelming majority after the BNP boycotted, extending HASINA's term as prime minister. With the help of international development assistance, Bangladesh has made great progress in food security since independence, and the economy has grown at an average of about 6 percent over the last two decades.

Chapter 2: Geography

Location:

Southern Asia, bordering the Bay of Bengal, between Burma and India

Geographic coordinates:

24 00 N, 90 00 E

Map references:

Asia

Area:

total: 143,998 sq km

country comparison to the world: 95

land: 130,168 sq km

water: 13,830 sq km

Area - comparative:

slightly smaller than Iowa

Land boundaries:

total: 4,246 km

border countries: Burma 193 km, India 4,053 km

Coastline:

580 km

Maritime claims:

territorial sea: 12 nm

contiguous zone: 18 nm

exclusive economic zone: 200 nm

continental shelf: up to the outer limits of the continental margin

Climate:

tropical; mild winter (October to March); hot, humid summer (March to June); humid, warm rainy monsoon (June to October)

Terrain:

mostly flat alluvial plain; hilly in southeast

Elevation extremes:

lowest point: Indian Ocean 0 m

highest point: Keokradong 1,230 m

Natural resources:

natural gas, arable land, timber, coal

Land use:

arable land: 52.97%

permanent crops: 6.25%

other: 40.78% (2011)

Irrigated land:

50,500 sq km (2008)

Total renewable water resources:

1,227 cu km (2011)

Freshwater withdrawal (domestic/industrial/agricultural):

total: 35.87 cu km/yr (10%/2%/88%)

per capita: 238.3 cu m/yr (2008)

Natural hazards:

droughts; cyclones; much of the country routinely inundated during the summer monsoon season

Environment - current issues:

many people are landless and forced to live on and cultivate flood-prone land; waterborne diseases prevalent in surface water; water pollution, especially of fishing areas, results from the use of commercial pesticides; ground water contaminated by naturally occurring arsenic; intermittent water shortages because of falling water tables in the northern and central parts of the country; soil degradation and erosion; deforestation; severe overpopulation

Environment - international agreements:

party to: Biodiversity, Climate Change, Climate Change-Kyoto Protocol, Desertification, Endangered Species, Environmental Modification, Hazardous Wastes, Law of the Sea, Ozone Layer Protection, Ship Pollution, Wetlands

signed, but not ratified: none of the selected agreements

Geography - note:

most of the country is situated on deltas of large rivers flowing from the Himalayas: the Ganges unites with the Jamuna (main channel of the Brahmaputra) and later joins the Meghna to eventually empty into the Bay of Bengal

Chapter 3: People and Society

Nationality:

noun: Bangladeshi(s)

adjective: Bangladeshi

Ethnic groups:

Bengali 98%, other 2% (includes tribal groups, non-Bengali Muslims) (1998)

Languages:

Bangla (official, also known as Bengali), English

Religions:

Muslim 89.5%, Hindu 9.6%, other 0.9% (2004)

Population:

166,280,712 (July 2014 est.)

country comparison to the world: 9

Age structure:

0-14 years: 32.3% (male 27,268,560/female 26,468,883)

15-24 years: 18.8% (male 14,637,526/female 16,630,766)

25-54 years: 38% (male 29,853,531/female 33,266,733)

55-64 years: 5% (male 4,964,130/female 4,870,447)

65 years and over: 4.9% (male 4,082,544/female 4,237,592) (2014 est.)

Dependency ratios:

> total dependency ratio: 53.3 %
>
> youth dependency ratio: 46 %
>
> elderly dependency ratio: 7.3 %
>
> potential support ratio: 13.6 (2013)

Median age:

> total: 24.3 years
>
> male: 23.8 years
>
> female: 24.8 years (2014 est.)

Population growth rate:

> 1.6% (2014 est.)
>
> country comparison to the world: 77

Birth rate:

> 21.61 births/1,000 population (2014 est.)
>
> country comparison to the world: 76

Death rate:

> 5.64 deaths/1,000 population (2014 est.)
>
> country comparison to the world: 175

Net migration rate:

> -0.02 migrant(s)/1,000 population (2014 est.)
>
> country comparison to the world: 110

Urbanization:

> urban population: 28.4% of total population (2011)
>
> rate of urbanization: 2.96% annual rate of change (2010-15 est.)

Major urban areas - population:

DHAKA (capital) 15.391 million; Chittagong 4.816 million; Khulna 1.636 million; Rajshahi 853,000 (2011)

Sex ratio:

at birth: 1.04 male(s)/female

0-14 years: 1.03 male(s)/female

15-24 years: 0.88 male(s)/female

25-54 years: 0.9 male(s)/female

55-64 years: 0.95 male(s)/female

65 years and over: 0.96 male(s)/female

total population: 0.95 male(s)/female (2014 est.)

Mother's mean age at first birth:

18.1

note: median age at first birth among women 25-29 (2011 est.)

Maternal mortality rate:

240 deaths/100,000 live births (2010)

country comparison to the world: 49

Infant mortality rate:

total: 45.67 deaths/1,000 live births

country comparison to the world: 45

male: 48.15 deaths/1,000 live births

female: 44.31 deaths/1,000 live births (2014 est.)

Life expectancy at birth:

    total population: 70.65 years

    country comparison to the world: 149

    male: 68.75 years

    female: 72.63 years (2014 est.)

Total fertility rate:

    2.45 children born/woman (2014 est.)

    country comparison to the world: 83

Contraceptive prevalence rate:

    61.2% (2011/12)

Health expenditures:

    3.7% of GDP (2011)

    country comparison to the world: 174

Physicians density:

    0.36 physicians/1,000 population (2011)

Hospital bed density:

    0.6 beds/1,000 population (2011)

Drinking water source:

    improved:

        urban: 85.3% of population

        rural: 82.4% of population

        total: 83.2% of population

    unimproved:

        urban: 14.7% of population

        rural: 17.6% of population

        total: 16.8% of population (2011 est.)

Sanitation facility access:

> improved:

>> *urban*: 55.3% of population

>> *rural*: 54.5% of population

>> *total*: 54.7% of population

> unimproved:

>> *urban*: 44.7% of population

>> *rural*: 45.5% of population

>> *total*: 45.3% of population (2011 est.)

HIV/AIDS - adult prevalence rate:

> 0.1% (2012 est.)

> country comparison to the world: 126

HIV/AIDS - people living with HIV/AIDS:

> 8,000 (2012 est.)

> country comparison to the world: 113

HIV/AIDS - deaths:

> 400 (2012 est.)

> country comparison to the world: 97

Major infectious diseases:

> degree of risk: high

> food or waterborne diseases: bacterial and protozoal diarrhea, hepatitis A and E, and typhoid fever

> vectorborne diseases: dengue fever and malaria are high risks in some locations

> water contact disease: leprospirosis

> animal contact disease: rabies

note: highly pathogenic H5N1 avian influenza has been identified in this country; it poses a negligible risk with extremely rare cases possible among US citizens who have close contact with birds (2013)

Obesity - adult prevalence rate:

1.1% (2008)

country comparison to the world: 190

Children under the age of 5 underweight:

36.8% (2011)

country comparison to the world: 5

Education expenditures:

2.2% of GDP (2009)

country comparison to the world: 161

Literacy:

definition: age 15 and over can read and write

total population: 57.7%

male: 62%

female: 53.4% (2011 est.)

School life expectancy (primary to tertiary education):

total: 10 years

male: 10 years

female: 10 years (2011)

Child labor – children ages 5-14:

total number: 4,485,497

percentage: 13 % (2006 est.)

Unemployment, youth ages 15-24:

> total: 9.3%
>
> country comparison to the world: 114
>
> male: 8%
>
> female: 13.6% (2005)

Chapter 4: Government and Key Leaders

Country name:

> conventional long form: People's Republic of Bangladesh
>
> conventional short form: Bangladesh
>
> local long form: Gana Prajatantri Bangladesh
>
> local short form: Bangladesh
>
> former: East Bengal, East Pakista

Government type:

> parliamentary democracy

Capital:

> name: Dhaka
>
> geographic coordinates: 23 43 N, 90 24 E
>
> time difference: UTC+6 (11 hours ahead of Washington, DC during Standard Time)

Administrative divisions:

> 7 divisions; Barisal, Chittagong, Dhaka, Khulna, Rajshahi, Rangpur, Sylhet

Independence:

> 16 December 1971 (from West Pakistan)

National holiday:

Independence Day, 26 March (1971); Victory Day; note - March 1971 is the date of the Awami League's declaration of an independent Bangladesh, and 16 December, known as Victory Day, memorializes the military victory over Pakistan and the official creation of the state of Bangladesh

Constitution:

previous 1935, 1956, 1962 (preindependence); latest enacted 4 November 1972, effective 16 December 1972, suspended March 1982, restored November 1986; amended many times, last in 2011 (2011)

Legal system:

mixed legal system of mostly English common law and Islamic law

International law organization participation:

has not submitted an ICJ jurisdiction declaration; accepts ICCt jurisdiction

Suffrage:

18 years of age; universal

Executive branch:

chief of state: President Abdul HAMID (since 24 April 2013); note - Abdul HAMID served as acting president following the death of Zillur RAHMAN in March 2013; HAMID was subsequently elected by the National Parliament and was sworn in 24 April 2013 head of government: Prime Minister Sheikh HASINA (since 6 January 2009; reelected 5 January 2014)

cabinet: Cabinet selected by the prime minister and appointed by the president

elections: president elected by National Parliament for a five-year term (eligible for a second term); last election held on 29 April 2013 (next must be held by 2018)

Legislative branch:

unicameral National Parliament or Jatiya Sangsad; 300 seats (45 reserved for women) elected by popular vote from single territorial constituencies; members serve five-year terms

elections: last held on 5 January 2014 (next to be held by January 2019); note - the 5 January 2014 poll was marred by widespread violence, boycotts, general strikes, and low voter turnout

election results: percent of vote by party - AL-led Alliance 77%, JP 33%; seats by party - AL 235, JP 34, other 28

Judicial branch:

Highest court(s): Supreme Court of Bangladesh (organized into the Appellate Division with 7 justices and the High Court Division with 99 justices)

Judge selection and term of offfice: chief justice and justices appointed by the president; justices serve until retirement at age 67 subordinate courts: civil courts include: Assistant Judge's Court; Joint District Judge's Court; Additional District Judge's Court; District Judge's Court; criminal courts include: Court of Sessions; Court of Metropolitan Sessions; special courts/tribunals; Metropolitan Magistrate Courts; Magistrate Court

Political parties and leaders:

> Awami League or AL [Sheikh HASINA]
>
> Communist Party of Bangladesh or CPB [Manjurul A. KHAN]
>
> Bangladesh Nationalist Front or BNF [Abdul Kalam AZADI]
>
> Bangladesh Nationalist Party or BNP [Khaleda ZIA]
>
> Bikalpa Dhara Bangladesh or BDB [Badrudozza CHOWDHURY]
>
> Islami Oikya Jote or IOJ [multiple leaders]
>
> Jatiya Party or JP (Ershad faction) [Hussain Mohammad ERSHAD]
>
> Liberal Democratic Party or LDP [Oli AHMED]
>
> National Socialist Party or JSD [KHALEQUZZAMAN]

Tarikat Foundation [Syed Nozibul Bashar
MAIZBHANDARI]
Workers Party or WP [Rashed Khan MENON]

Political pressure groups and leaders:

Advocacy to End Gender-based Violence through the
MoWCA (Ministry of Women's and Children's
Affairs)
Ain o Salish Kendro (Law and Order Center)
Bangladesh Rural Advancement Committee or BRAC
Bangladesh Center for Worker Solidarity
Federation of Bangladesh Chambers of Commerce
and Industry
Odikhar (Human Rights)

other: human rights organizations; vendors

International organization participation:

ADB, ARF, ASEAN, CICA, CICA (observer), EAS, FAO,
G-77, IAEA, IBRD, ICAO, ICRM, IDA, IFAD, IFC,
IFRCS, ILO, IMF, IMO, Interpol, IOC, IOM, IPU, ISO
(correspondent), ITU, MINUSMA, MIGA, NAM, OIF,
OPCW, PCA, UN, UNCTAD, UNESCO, UNIDO,
UNIFIL, UNMISS, UNWTO, UPU, WCO, WFTU
(NGOs), WHO, WIPO, WMO, WTO

Diplomatic representation in the US:

chief of mission: Ambassador Akramul QADER (since 1 September 2009)

chancery: 3510 International Drive NW, Washington, DC 20008

telephone: [1] (202) 244-0183

FAX: [1] (202) 244-7830/2771

consulate(s) general: Los Angeles, New York

Diplomatic representation from the US:

chief of mission: Ambassador Dan W. MOZENA (since 11 November 2011)

embassy: Madani Avenue, Baridhara, Dhaka 1212

mailing address: G. P. O. Box 323, Dhaka 1000

telephone: [880] (2) 885-5500

FAX: [880] (2) 882-3744

Key Leaders:

Pres.	Abdul HAMID
Prime Min.	Sheikh HASINA
Min. of Agriculture	Matia CHOWDHURY
Min. of Civil Aviation & Tourism	Rashed Khan MENON
Min. of Commerce	Tofail AHMED
Min. of Communications	Obaidul QUADER
Min. of Cultural Affairs	Asaduzzaman NOOR
Min. of Defense	Sheikh HASINA
Min. of Disaster Management & Relief	Mofazzal Hossain Chowdhury MAYA
Min. of Education	Nurul Islam NAHID
Min. of Environment & Forest	Anwar Hossain MONJU

Min. of Expatriates' Welfare & Overseas Employment	Khandaker Mosharraf HOSSAIN
Min. of Finance	Abu Maal Abdul MUHITH
Min. of Fisheries & Livestock	Sayedul HAQUE
Min. of Food	Qamrul ISLAM
Min. of Foreign Affairs	AH Mahmood Ali
Min. of Health & Family Planning	Mohammad NASIM
Min. of Home Affairs	
Min. of Housing & Public Works	Mosharraf HOSSAIN
Min. of Industries	Amir Hossain AMU
Min. of Information	Hasanul Haq INU
Min. of Information & Communication Technology	Abdul Latif SIDDIQUE
Min. of Labor & Employment	Mujibul Haque CHUNNU
Min. of Land	Shamsher Rahman SHARIF
Min. of Law	Anisul HAQUE
Min of Liberation War	AKM Mojammel HAQUE
Min. of Local Govt., Rural Development, & Cooperatives	Syed Ashraful ISLAM
Min. of Planning	AHM Mostafa KAMAL
Min. of Posts & Telecommunications	Abdul Latif SIDDIQUE
Min. of Power, Energy, & Mineral Resources	
Min. of Primary & Mass Education	Mustafizur Rahman FIZAR
Min. of Public Admin.	Sheikh HASINA
Min. of Railways	Mujibul HUQ
Min. of Religious Affairs	Motiur RAHMAN
Min. of Rural Development & Cooperatives	Moshiur Rahman RANGA
Min. of Science & Technology	
Min. of Shipping	Shahjahan KHAN
Min. of Social Welfare	Syed Mohsin ALI

Min. of Textiles & Jute	Emajuddin PRAMANIK
Min. of Water Resources	Anisul Islam MAHMUD
Governor, Bangladesh Bank	Atiur RAHMAN
Ambassador to the US	Akramul QADER
Permanent Representative to the UN, New York	Abdulkalam Abdul MOMEN

Flag description:

green field with a large red disk shifted slightly to the hoist side of center; the red disk represents the rising sun and the sacrifice to achieve independence; the green field symbolizes the lush vegetation of Bangladesh

National symbol(s):

Bengal tiger, water lily

National anthem:

name: "Amar Shonar Bangla" (My Golden Bengal)

lyrics/music: Rabindranath TAGORE

note: adopted 1971; Rabindranath TAGORE, a Nobel laureate, also wrote India's national anthem

Chapter 5: Economy

Economy - overview:

Bangladesh's economy has grown roughly 6% per year since 1996 despite political instability, poor infrastructure, corruption, insufficient power supplies, slow implementation of economic reforms, and the 2008-09 global financial crisis and recession. Although more than half of GDP is generated through the service sector, almost half of Bangladeshis are employed in the agriculture sector with rice as the single-most-important product. Garment exports, the backbone of Bangladesh's industrial sector and 80% of total exports, surpassed $21 billion last year, 18% of GDP. The sector has remained resilient in recent years amidst a series of factory accidents that have killed over 1,000 workers and crippling strikes that shut down virtually all economic activity. Steady garment export growth combined with remittances from overseas Bangladeshis, which totaled almost $15 billion and 13% of GDP IN 2013, are the largest contributors to Bangladesh's current account surplus and record foreign exchange holdings.

GDP (purchasing power parity):

$324.6 billion (2013 est.)

country comparison to the world: 44

$307 billion (2012 est.)

$289.2 billion (2011 est.)

note: data are in 2013 US dollars

GDP (official exchange rate):

$140.2 billion (2013 est.)

GDP - real growth rate:

5.8% (2013 est.)

country comparison to the world: 40

6.1% (2012 est.)

6.5% (2011 est.)

GDP - per capita (PPP):

$2,100 (2013 est.)

country comparison to the world: 194

$2,000 (2012 est.)

$1,900 (2011 est.)

note: data are in 2013 US dollars

Gross national saving:

28.3% of GDP (2013 est.)

country comparison to the world: 34

27% of GDP (2012 est.)

25% of GDP (2011 est.)

GDP – composition, by end use:

household consumption: 75.3%

government consumption: 5.7%

investment in fixed capital: 25.6%

investment in inventories: 3.6%

exports of goods and services: 24.5%

imports of goods and services: -34.7% (2013 est.)

GDP - composition by sector:

agriculture: 17.2%

industry: 28.9%

services: 53.9% (2013 est.)

Agriculture – products:

rice, jute, tea, wheat, sugarcane, potatoes, tobacco, pulses, oilseeds, spices, fruit; beef, milk, poultry

Industries:

jute, cotton, garments, paper, leather, fertilizer, iron and steel, cement, petroleum products, tobacco, drugs and pharmaceuticals, ceramics, tea, salt, sugar, edible oils, soap and detergent, fabricated metal products, electricity and natural gas

Industrial production growth rate:

9% (2013 est.)

country comparison to the world: 20

Labor force:

78.62 million

country comparison to the world: 7

extensive export of labor to Saudi Arabia, Kuwait, UAE,
Oman, Qatar, and Malaysia; workers' remittances were
$10.9 billion in FY09/10 (2013 est.)

Labor force - by occupation:

agriculture: 47%

industry: 13%

services: 40% (2010 est.)

Unemployment rate:

5% (2013 est.)

country comparison to the world: 48

5% (2012 est.)

note: about 40% of the population is underemployed;
many participants in the labor force work only a few hours
a week, at low wages

Population below poverty line:

31.5% (2010 est.)

Household income or consumption by percentage share:

lowest 10%: 4%

highest 10%: 27% (2010 est.)

Distribution of family income - Gini index:

32.1 (2010)

country comparison to the world: 105

33.6 (1996)

Budget:

revenues: $17.19 billion

expenditures: $24.02 billion (2013 est.)

Taxes and other revenues:

12.3% of GDP (2013 est.)

country comparison to the world: 202

Budget surplus (+) or deficit (-):

-4.9% of GDP (2013 est.)

country comparison to the world: 163

Public debt:

30.9% of GDP (2013 est.)

country comparison to the world: 118

32.2% of GDP (2012 est.)

Inflation rate (consumer prices):

7.6% (2013 est.)

country comparison to the world: 190

6.6% (2012 est.)

Central bank discount rate:

5% (31 December 2010 est.)

country comparison to the world: 70

5% (31 December 2009 est.)

Commercial bank prime lending rate:

13% (31 December 2013 est.)

country comparison to the world: 60

13% (31 December 2012 est.)

Stock of narrow money:

$17.11 billion (31 December 2013 est.)

country comparison to the world: 68

$14.85 billion (31 December 2012 est.)

Stock of broad money:

$85.61 billion (31 December 2013 est.)

country comparison to the world: 58

$70.87 billion (31 December 2012 est.)

Stock of domestic credit:

$93.38 billion (31 December 2013 est.)

country comparison to the world: 54

$79.32 billion (31 December 2012 est.)

Market value of publicly traded shares:

$37.34 billion (February 2014 est.)

country comparison to the world: 64

$17.48 billion (31 December 2012)

$23.55 billion (31 December 2011 est.)

Current account balance:

$3.541 billion (2013 est.)

country comparison to the world: 32

$1.754 billion (2012 est.)

Exports:

$26.91 billion (2013 est.)

country comparison to the world: 68

$24.92 billion (2012 est.)

Exports - commodities:

garments, knitwear, agricultural products, frozen food (fish and seafood), jute and jute goods, leather

Exports - partners:

US 18.7%, Germany 15.8%, UK 10.2%, France 6.2%, Spain 4.6%, Canada 4.3%, Italy 4% (2013 est.)

Imports:

$32.94 billion (2013 est.)

country comparison to the world: 64

$32.29 billion (2012 est.)

Imports - commodities:

machinery and equipment, chemicals, iron and steel, textiles, foodstuffs, petroleum products, cement

Imports - partners:

China 21.7%, India 16.3%, Malaysia 5.2%, Republic of Korea 4.5%, Japan 4.1% (2013 est.)

Reserves of f oreign exchange and gold:

$15.74 billion (31 December 2013 est.)

country comparison to the world: 68

$12.75 billion (31 December 2012 est.)

Debt - external:

$30.69 billion (31 December 2013 est.)

country comparison to the world: 72

$29.53 billion (31 December 2012 est.)

Stock of direct foreign investment – at home:

$7.04 billion (31 December 2013 est.)

country comaprison to the world: 87

$6.64 billion (31 December 2012 est.)

Stock of direct foreign investment – abroad:

$110.1 million (31 December 2013 est.)

country comparison ot the world: 86

$108.1 million (31 December 2012 est.)

Exchange rates:

taka (BDT) per US dollar –

78.19 (2013 est.)

81.863 (2012 est.)

69.649 (2010 est.)

69.04 (2009)

68.554 (2008)

Chapter 6: Energy

Electricity - production:

40.08 billion kWh (2011 est.)

country comparison to the world: 59

Electricity - consumption:

38.89 billion kWh (2010 est.)

country comparison to the world: 54

Electricity - exports:

0 kWh (2012 est.)

country comparison to the world: 105

Electricity - imports:

500,000 kWh (2013 est.)

country comparison to the world: 107

Electricity - installed generating capacity:

10.26 million kW (2013 est.)

country comparison to the world: 53

Electricity - from fossil fuels:

97.7% of total installed capacity (2013 est.)

country comparison to the world: 60

Electricity - from nuclear fuels:

0% of total installed capacity (2013 est.)

country comparison to the world: 48

Electricity - from hydroelectric plants:

2.3% of total installed capacity (2013 est.)

country comparison to the world: 134

Electricity - from other renewable sources:

0% of total installed capacity (2013 est.)

country comparison to the world: 157

Crude oil - production:

5,452 bbl/day (2012 est.)

country comparison to the world: 97

Crude oil - exports:

0 bbl/day (2010 est.)

country comparison to the world: 84

Crude oil - imports:

23,620 bbl/day (2010 est.)

country comparison to the world: 66

Crude oil - proved reserves:

28 million bbl (1 January 2013 es)

country comparison to the world: 82

Refined petroleum products - production:

22,710 bbl/day (2010 est.)

country comparison to the world: 90

Refined petroleum products - consumption:

108,900 bbl/day (2011 est.)

country comparison to the world: 74

Refined petroleum products - exports:

3,288 bbl/day (2010 est.)

country comparison to the world: 97

Refined petroleum products - imports:

> 84,490 bbl/day (2010 est.)

> country comparison to the world: 54

Natural gas - production:

> 20.11 billion cu m (2011 est.)

> country comparison to the world: 32

Natural gas - consumption:

> 19.91 billion cu m (2010 est.)

> country comparison to the world: 35

Natural gas - exports:

> 0 cu m (2011 est.)

> country comparison to the world: 65

Natural gas - imports:

> 0 cu m (2011 est.)

> country comparison to the world: 160

Natural gas - proved reserves:

> 183.7 billion cu m (1 January 2013 es)

> country comparison to the world: 47

Carbon dioxide emissions from consumption of energy:

> 58.81 million Mt (2011 est.)

> country comparison to the world: 56

Chapter 7: Communications

Telephones - main lines in use:

> 962,000 (2012)

> country comparison to the world: 78

Telephones - mobile cellular:

> 97.18 million (2011)

> country comparison to the world: 15

Telephone system:

> general assessment: inadequate for a modern country; introducing digital systems; trunk systems include VHF and UHF microwave radio relay links, and some fiber-optic cable in cities

> domestic: fixed-line teledensity remains only about 1 per 100 persons; mobile-cellular telephone subscribership has been increasing rapidly and now exceeds 50 telephones per 100 persons

> international: country code - 880; landing point for the SEA-ME-WE-4 fiber-optic submarine cable system that provides links to Europe, the Middle East, and Asia; satellite earth stations - 6; international radiotelephone communications and landline service to neighboring countries (2011)

Broadcast media:

state-owned Bangladesh Television (BTV) operates 1 terrestrial TV station, 3 radio networks, and about 10 local stations; 8 private satellite TV stations and 3 private radio stations also broadcasting; foreign satellite TV stations are gaining audience share in the large cities; several international radio broadcasters are available (2007)

Internet country code:

.bd

Internet hosts:

71,164 (2012)

country comparison to the world: 87

Internet users:

617,300 (2009)

country comparison to the world: 112

Chapter 8: Transportation

Airports:

18 (2013)

country comparison to the world: 139

Airports - with paved runways:

total: 16

over 3,047 m: 2

2,438 to 3,047 m: 2

1,524 to 2,437 m: 6

914 to 1,523 m: 1

under 914 m: 5 (2013)

Airports - with unpaved runways:

total: 2

1,524 to 2,437 m: 1

under 914 m: 1 (2013)

Heliports:

3 (2013)

Pipelines:

gas 2,950 km (2013)

Railways:

total: 2,622 km

country comparison to the world: 65

broad gauge: 946 km 1.676-m gauge

narrow gauge: 1,676 km 1.000-m gauge (2008)

Roadways:

    total: 21,269 km

    country comparison to the world: 106

    paved: 1,063 km

    unpaved: 20,206 km (2010)

Waterways:

    8,370 km (includes up to 3,060 km of main cargo routes;

    the network is reduced to 5,200 km in the dry season)

    (2011)

    country comparison to the world: 17

Merchant marine:

    total: 62

    country comparison to the world: 64

    by type: bulk carrier 25, cargo 28, chemical tanker 1,

    container 5, petroleum tanker 3

    foreign-owned: 8 (China 1, Singapore 7)

    registered in other countries: 10 (Comoros 1, Hong Kong 1,

    Panama 5, Saint Vincent and the Grenadines 1, Sierra

    Leone 1, Singapore 1) (2010)

Ports and terminals:

    major seaport(s): Chittagong

    river port(s): Mongla Port (Sela River)

    container port(s): Chittagong (1,392,104) (2011)

Transportation – note:

the International Maritime Bureau reports the territorial waters of Bangladesh remain a risk for armed robbery against ships; attacks against vessels have decreased over the last few years in response to improved local security

Chapter 9: Military

Military branches:

Bangladesh Defense Force: Bangladesh Army (Sena Bahini), Bangladesh Navy (Noh Bahini, BN), Bangladesh Air Force (Biman Bahini, BAF) (2013)

Military service age and obligation:

16-19 years of age for voluntary military service; Bangladeshi birth and 10th grade education required; initial obligation 15 years (2012)

Manpower available for military service:

males age 16-49: 36,520,491 (2010 est.)

Manpower fit for military service:

males age 16-49: 30,486,086

females age 16-49: 35,616,093 (2010 est.)

Manpower reaching militarily significant age annually:

male: 1,606,963

female: 1,689,442 (2010 est.)

Military expenditures:

1.35% of GDP (2012)

country comparison to the world: 76

1.44% of GDP (2011)

1.35% of GDP (2010)

Chapter 10: Transnational Issues

Disputes - international:

Bangladesh referred its maritime boundary claims with Burma and India to the International Tribunal on the Law of the Sea; Indian Prime Minister Singh's September 2011 visit to Bangladesh resulted in the signing of a Protocol to the 1974 Land Boundary Agreement between India and Bangladesh, which had called for the settlement of longstanding boundary disputes over undemarcated areas and the exchange of territorial enclaves, but which had never been implemented; Bangladesh struggles to accommodate 29,000 Rohingya, Burmese Muslim minority from Arakan State, living as refugees in Cox's Bazar; Burmese border authorities are constructing a 200 km (124 mi) wire fence designed to deter illegal cross-border transit and tensions from the military build-up along border

Refugees and internally displaced persons:

refugees (country of origin): 230,674 (Burma) (2012)

IDPs: undetermined (land conflicts, religious persecution) (2012)

Illicit drugs:

transit country for illegal drugs produced in neighboring countries

Map of Bangladesh

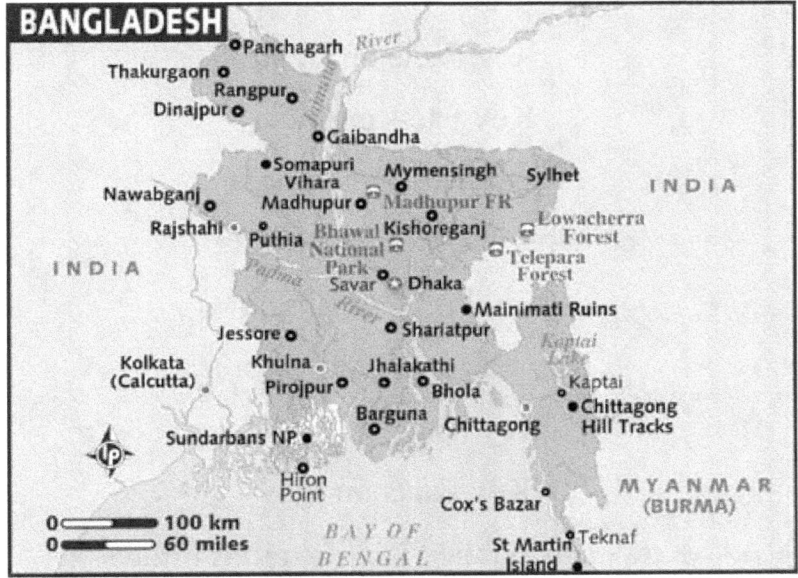

Other Key Facts™ Titles

Key Facts on Syria

Key Facts on China

Key Facts on Qatar

Key Facts on India

Key Facts on Germany

Key Facts on Argentina

Key Facts on Russia

Key Facts on North Korea

Key Facts on Brazil

Key Facts on Italy

Key Facts on the United Arab Emirates

Key Facts on the European Union

Key Facts on Pakistan

Key Facts on Saudi Arabia

Key Facts on Cyprus

Key Facts on Iran

Key Facts on Afghanistan

Key Facts on Iraq

Key Facts on Indonesia

Key Facts on South Korea

Key Facts on France

Key Facts on the United Kingdom

Key Facts on Egypt

Key Facts on Israel

All Key Facts™ Titles are Available at

www.Amazon.com

THE INTERNATIONALIST®

2014

WWW.INTERNATIONALIST.COM

www.ingramcontent.com/pod-product-compliance
Lightning Source LLC
Chambersburg PA
CBHW071829170526
45167CB00003B/1470